S0-BBB-602

世界遗产

苏州古典园林

THE CLASSICAL GARDENS OF SUZHOU, THE WORLD HERITAGE

苏州市园林管理局 编

上海三联书店

图书在版编目(CIP)数据

苏州古典园林: 汉英对照／苏州市园林管理局编

上海: 上海三联书店,2000.1

ISBN7-5426-1327-8

Ⅰ.苏…

Ⅱ.苏…

Ⅲ.古典园林－江苏－苏州市郊－摄影集…

Ⅳ.TU986..625.33-64…

中国版本图书馆 CIP 数据核字(1999)第 77280 号

《苏州古典园林》

编委会主任　徐文涛

编　　委	徐文涛	程伯寿	吴素芬	茅晓伟	张树多
	黄敬如	徐春明	周健生	周苏宁	周　峥
	潘益新	卢彩萍	方佩和	孙志勤	刘　苏
	游伟刚	陈　中	高云根	宋月圆	

撰　　文　周　峥

摄　　影　金宝源

　　　　　方佩和　缪立群　项联元

编　辑　部

责任编辑　朱国安　张　英

特约编辑　周苏宁　周　峥

美术编辑　鲁继德

装帧设计　鲁继德

英文翻译　董晓明(English: Dong Xiaoming)

编　　务　沈　亮　吴春秋

书　　名　苏州古典园林

出　　版　上海三联书店

(200233)中国上海市钦州南路81号

发　　行　新华书店上海发行所

　　　　　上海三联书店

制　　版　蛇口以琳彩印制版有限公司

印刷装订　东莞新扬印刷有限公司

版　　次　2000年1月第1版

印　　次　2000年1月第1次印刷

开　　本　787×1092 1/8

印　　张　6

印　　数　1-3500

书　　号　ISBN7-5426-1327-8/J·60

定　　价　60元

苏州是一座具有 2500 余年历史的文化古城,地处长江下游的太湖之滨,自然条件和地理环境十分优越。自公元前 514 年建城,这里一直是江南地区的重镇;特别是明清以来,工商繁荣,人文荟萃,成为中国经济文化中心,尤其是建筑、绘画、戏曲、工艺美术和文学创作等方面,水平高超,名家辈出。

在优越的自然条件、地理环境和浓郁的文化氛围中,苏州产生了如诗如画的古典园林。其数量之多,艺术之精,文化内涵之丰,不仅独步江南,而且誉满中外,是我国传统文化中的瑰宝。

苏州古典园林的历史可上溯至公元前 6 世纪吴王的苑囿。私家园林最早见于记载的是东晋(4 世纪)的辟疆园。16 世纪至 18 世纪,苏州造园达到全盛时期,私家园林遍布古城内外。据记载,当时有园林二百余处,现保存完好的尚有数十处。

苏州古典园林运用中国独特的造园手法,在城市住宅旁有限的空间里,通过叠山理水,栽植花木,营构建筑,创造出充满诗情画意的文人写意山水园林。这些充满自然意趣的"城市山林",在都市内营造了人与自然和谐相处的环境,表现出古人崇尚自然、回归自然的愿望。今天,我们从园林的山水花木中,从园林的景点题名上,仍能看到造园者追崇自然的文化心态。

苏州园林是中国园林历史的实证,是中国造园艺术的典范,是中国园林理论研究的重要范本。"中国是世界造园之母,苏州园林是中国园林的杰出代表",这一古人留下的财富,经一代代先人的努力保护,经今人的精心管理,其多重价值,正为人们日益深刻地认识。

1997 年 12 月 4 日,联合国教科文组织遗产委员会第 21 届会议批准,以拙政园、留园、网师园、环秀山庄为典型例证的苏州古典园林列入《世界遗产名录》。1998 年 12 月,经中华人民共和国国务院批准,沧浪亭、狮子林、艺圃、耦园、退思园作为世界遗产——苏州古典园林的增补名单,正式呈报联合国教科文组织。

徐文涛

PREFACE

With favorable natural and geographic conditions and a history of more than 2, 500 years, Suzhou is a historic and cultural city situated in the Lower Yangtze basin by the side of Lake Tai. Founded in 514 B. C. Suzhou has been an important metropolis in the area south of the Lower Yangtze. Ever since the Ming and Qing Dynasties, Suzhou, noted for its well – known scholars, great artists, outstanding architects, prominent playwrights and literary men, has beheld the prosperity of its industries and commerce, becoming the economic and cultural center of China. Under these advantageous circumstances, the classical gardens of Suzhou came into being. Famous at home and abroad, they are poetic, picturesque, numerous, exquisite and rich in literary connotations, and represent themselves as a brilliant gem of Chinese cultural heritage

The earliest gardens of Suzhou, which belonged to the King of Wu, can be traced far back to the 6th century B. C. The Pijiang Garden was recorded as the earliest privately – owned garden dating from the 4th century Eastern Jin Dynasty. Historical records show that the classical gardens of Suzhou reached their apogee in a period of time from the 16th to the 18th century and more than 200 gardens were built in the city of Suzhou and its environs. Dozens of them have survived to the present day and are kept in a good state of preservation.

Laid out within a limited area by the house, a classical garden of Suzhou is a microcosm of the world made of the basic elements of water, rocks, vegetation and various kinds of buildings. Like the freehand brushwork in traditional Chinese painting, it is the creation of "urban scenery" or an amicable environment that brings man into harmony with nature. The Chinese ancients held Mother Nature in reverence and had a desire to return to her arms. Today, we can discover these cultural mentalities by observing the landscapes, waterscapes, vegetation and inscriptions of the existing gardens.

The classical gardens of Suzhou, bearing unambiguous evidence of the evolution of Chinese gardens, are excellent examples of Chinese landscape gardening and important models for garden theoretical researches. "Chinese gardens are the mother of gardens on earth and Suzhou gardens are the brilliant representatives of Chinese gardens." Viewed in broad perspectives, people are becoming aware of the value of these treasures handed down from the past generations to the present with protective measures and great care.

On Dec. 4, 1997, the 21st session of the UNESCO World Heritage Committee was unanimous in support of the decision of inscribing on the World Heritage List the classical gardens of Suzhou with the Humble Administrator's Garden, the Lingering Garden, the Master – of – Nets Garden and the Mountain Villa with Embracing Beauty as the finest specimens. In Dec. 1998, the State Council of the People's Republic of China approved of putting the Canglang Pavilion, the Lion Forest Garden, the Garden of Cultivation, the Couple's Garden Retreat and the Retreat & Reflection Garden on A Supplementary List of the Classical Gardens of Suzhou – the World Heritage and officially submitted it to United Nations Educational, Scientific and Cultural Organization (UNESCO).

Chineseby: Xu Wentao

TABLE OF CONTENTS 目录

拙政园   8

留园   14

网师园   20

环秀山庄   24

沧浪亭   28

狮子林   32

艺圃   36

耦园   40

退思园   44

THE HUMBLE ADMINISTRATOR'S GARDEN   8

THE LINGERING GARDEN   14

THE MASTER – OF – NETS GARDEN   20

THE MOUNTAIN VILLA WITH EMBRACING BEAUTY   24

THE CANGLANG PAVILION   28

THE LION FOREST GARDEN   32

THE GARDEN OF CULTIVATION   36

THE COUPLE'S GARDEN RETREAT   40

THE RETREAT & REFLECTION GARDEN   44

1

拙政园

THE HUMBLE ADMINISTRATOR'S GARDEN

拙政园位于苏州古城东北部,占地 5.2 公顷,是苏州古典园林的代表作,也是中国四大名园之一。1961 年被列为全国重点文物保护单位;1997 年与留园、网师园、环秀山庄一起作为苏州古典园林的典型例证,被联合国教科文组织列入《世界遗产名录》。始建于明代正德四年(1509),御使王献臣遭贬回乡建造,取晋代潘岳《闲居赋》"灌园鬻蔬,以供朝夕之膳,……是亦拙者之为政也"语意命名。现园分东、中、西和住宅部分:东部原名"归田园居",中部为全园的精华所在,西部是清光绪年重修的"补园",三处历史上曾一度分开,50 年代重又合并向公众开放。拙政园布局因地制宜,以水为中心,各式建筑缘水而筑,格调古朴自然,充满诗情画意,呈现出池广树茂、旷远明瑟的明代江南园林风格。园西部有盆景园,陈列苏派盆景 700 余盆。住宅部分现为苏州园林博物馆。每年春、夏季节举办杜鹃花展和荷花节。

2

Situated in the northeastern part of the ancient city of Suzhou, the Humble Administrator's Garden, covering 5.2 ha., is regarded as a typical example of the classical gardens of Suzhou and one of the four most famous gardens of China. In 1961 it was listed as cultural relics of national importance. Since 1997 the Humble Administrator's Garden, the Lingering Garden, the Master — of — Nets Garden and the Mountain Villa with Embracing Beauty, serving as the four finest specimens of the classical gardens of Suzhou, have been inscribed on the World Heritage List by UNESCO.

In the 4th year of the reign of Zhengde (A.D. 1509) under the Ming Dynasty, the Imperial Inspector Wang Xianchen returned to Suzhou after relegation and built his garden. He borrowed the idea from the essay entitled "Staying at Home Idle" by the Jin writer Pan Yue, saying, "To cultivate my garden and sell my vegetable crop ... is the policy of humble man." Hence the name. Now it consists of the housing complex, the eastern, middle and western parts. The eastern part was originally called the Retirement Farmhouse. The middle part is the cream of the whole garden. Reconstructed in the reign of Guangxu under the Qing Dynasty, the former Complementary Garden is to be found in the western part. Separated in the past, the three parts have been united and open to the public since the 1950s. Making good use of the natural contours, the Humble Administrator's Garden is centered upon the broad expanse of a lake with a variety of buildings constructed close to the water and exuberant bushes and trees. Its poetic and picturesque landscapes and waterscapes are described as being simple, archaic, extensive and natural, possessing the characteristics of the Ming style garden in the area south of the Lower Yangtze. There's a bonsai garden in the western part of the garden. A collection of over 700 Suzhou style bonsai is displayed there. Part of the housing complex is now used as the Suzhou Garden Museum. Rhododendron Simsii & R. Spp. Show in the spring and Nelumbo Nucifera Festival in the summer are held within the Humble Administrator's Garden.

4

5

1. 与谁同坐轩
2. 荷风四面亭
3. 见山楼西侧爬山廊
4. 绣绮亭
5. 倚玉轩
6. 小飞虹

1. The "With Whom Shall I Sit?" Pavilion
2. The Pavilion in Lotus Breezes
3. The Roofed Walkway Going Up the Mountain to the West of the Mountain – in – View Tower
4. The Peony Pavilion
5. The Bamboo Pavilion
6. The Small Flying Rainbow Bridge

6

玉蘭堂

1

2   3

4

1. 玉兰堂
2. 住宅墙门
3. 波形水廊
4. 远香堂陈设
5. 见山楼
6. 卅六鸳鸯馆窗影

1. The Magnolia Hall
2. The Entrance to the House
3. The Wavy Corridor over the Water
4. Furnishings of the Hall of Drifting Fragrance
5. The Mountain – in – View Tower
6. Window Pictures of the 36 Pairs of Mandarin Ducks' Hall

5

6

1

2

3

4

5

1. 香洲
2. 玲珑馆
3. 远眺北寺塔
4. 远香堂
5. 卅六鸳鸯馆
6. 海棠春坞

1. The Fragrant Isle
2. The Elegant Bamboo House
3. A Distant View of the North Temple Pagoda
4. The Hall of Drifting Fragrance
5. The 36 Pairs of Mandarin Duks' Hall
6. The Malus Micromalus Makina Court

6

留园

THE LINGERING GARDEN

1

留园位于苏州阊门外,占地2.3公顷,是中国四大名园之一,被誉为"吴中名园之冠"。1961年被列为全国重点文物保护单位;1997年与拙政园、网师园、环秀山庄一起作为苏州古典园林的典型例证,被联合国教科文组织列入《世界遗产名录》。始建于明万历年间,太仆徐泰时置东、西两园(后西园改为寺院),并请名师堆叠假山。清嘉庆年间,改名寒碧庄,又集湖石名峰十二峰于园内。同治末重修,改名留园。现园分东、中、西、北四部分,东部以庭院、建筑取胜;中部是山水写意园;西部林木幽深,有山林野趣;北部竹篱小屋,呈田园风貌。留园以建筑空间艺术处理精湛著称,园以厅堂、走廊、粉墙、洞门划分空间,通过与山水花木组合成一个个错落相联、层次丰富的庭院,体现了江南园林建筑的艺术特点。

Located at the outer side of the Chang Gate, the Lingering Garden, covering 2.3 ha., ranks first among all well—known gardens of Suzhou and is one of the four most famous gardens of China. In 1961 it was listed as cultural relics of national importance. Since 1997 the Lingering Garden, the Humble Administrator's Garden, the Master—of—Nets Garden and the Mountain Villa with Embracing Beauty, serving as the finest specimens of the classical gardens of Suzhou, have been inscribed on the World Heritage List by UNESCO.

In the 21st year of the reign of Wanli (A.D. 1593) under the Ming Dynasty, Xu Taishi, carrying the ministerial title of Tai Pu, built the East Garden and the West Garden (the West Garden Temple). A mountain range was piled up by the landscape master of the time. During the reign of Jiaqing it was renamed the Hanbi Villa. 12 famous limestone peaks from Lake Tai have added to the attraction of the garden since then. In the 12th year of the reign of Tongzhi it was repaired and took the present name. The Lingering Garden is now divided into four parts: the eastern, middle, western and northern parts. The eastern part features a happy grouping of exquisite buildings and garden courts. The middle part has a prominent area for its landscape garden which resembles freehand brushwork in traditional Chinese painting. The western part is noted for its delights of woody hills and wilderness, and the northern part its idyllic scenes and fenced small houses. The Lingering Garden is celebrated for its artistic way of dealing with the spaces between various kinds of architectural forms. The white—washed wall pierced with gates, roofed walkways, rooms and halls are not only the devices for separating different areas but also have combined with rockery, water—courses, trees and flowers, forming seemingly endless varieties of mini—gardens and demonstrating the artistic features of garden buildings in the area south of the Lower Yangtze.

2

3

4

5

1. 岫云峰
2. 曲溪楼
3. 明代花台
4. 怡航陈设
5. 东山丝竹
6. 石林小院

1. The Mountainous Cloud Peak
2. The Winding Stream Tower
3. The Flower – Bed of the Ming
4. Furnishings of the Pellucid Tower and the Inscription "Suitable for Boating"
5. The Hermit Music
6. The Small Garden Court of Stone Forest

1

1. 小蓬莱
2. 明瑟楼
3. 山水秋色
4. 冠云峰
5. 角隅配植
6. 爬山廊
7. 花步小筑

1. The Small Fairly Isle
2. The Pellucid Tower
3. The Autumnal Landscape and Waterscape
4. The Cloud – Capped Peak
5. Vegetation at the Garden Corner
6. The Roofed Walkway Going Up the Mountain
7. A Small Structure of Huabu

2   4

3

6

7

1

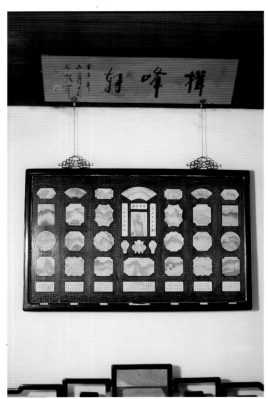

2

3

1. 五峰仙馆
2. 揖峰轩什锦挂屏
3. 林泉耆硕之馆
4. 五峰仙馆内陈设
5. 大理石座屏

1. The Celestial Hall of Five Peaks
2. Assorted Wall – Hangings in the Worshipping Stone Pavilion
3. The Old Hermit Scholars' House
4. Furnishings of the Celestial Hall of Five Peaks
5. The Marble Decoration

网师园

THE MASTER—OF—NETS GARDEN

网师园位于苏州古城东南隅,占地 0.6 公顷,布局精妙,被称为苏州小园林的极则,也是中国园林"以少胜多"的典范。1982 年被列为全国重点文物保护单位;1997 年作为苏州古典园林的典型例证,与拙政园、留园、环秀山庄一起被联合国教科文组织列入《世界遗产名录》。南宋侍郎史正志最早在这里建造万卷堂,堂侧建花园"渔隐"。清乾隆年间,宋氏购得后重新浚池叠石,筑堂构室,沿史氏"渔隐"义,名网师园。网师园保持了苏州旧时家完整的宅、园相连风貌,全园分为东部住宅区,中部山水花园、西部别院。东部厅堂布局严整,结构轩昂,装修雅洁;中部池水清澄,假山雄峻,亭台楼阁环池而筑;西部殿春簃,原为书院,80 年代初中国赴美国建造的纽约大都会艺术博物馆内的"明轩",即以此为蓝本。

With an area of 0.6 ha. and noted for its subtlety and compactness, the Master — of — Nets Garden, carefully planned and thoughtfully laid out at the southeastern corner of the ancient city of Suzhou, is indeed a good example of how the small garden exceeds the large and how the few surpasses the many in the Chinese garden. In 1982 it was listed as cultural relics of national importance. Since 1997 the Master — of — Nets Garden, the Humble Administrator's Garden, the Lingering Garden and the Mountain Villa with Embracing Beauty, regarded as representatives of the classical gardens of Suzhou, have been placed on the World Heritage List by UNESCO.

As early as the Southern Song Dynasty the Deputy Minister Shi Zhengzhi built the Hall of 10,000 Volumes in this place with a nearby garden known as the Fisherman's Retreat. In the reign of Qianlong, Song Zongyuan purchased it, rebuilt his landscape garden—house, borrowed the meaning of the Fisherman's Retreat and renamed it the Master—of—Nets Garden. Like most of the classical gardens of Suzhou belonging to noble families in olden times, the outstanding feature of this garden is that it is combined with the living quarters. The Master—of—Nets Garden consists of the eastern housing area, the central landscape garden and the western garden court. Constructed in accordance with the strict regulations, rooms and halls on the east are magnificent buildings with extraordinary furnishings and interior decoration. The central landscape garden features awe — inspiring man — made mountains and the pure expanse of a little lake surrounded by pavilions, terraces, towers and other forms of buildings. In the early 1980s a cadre of Chinese garden builders arrived at New York City, assembled a unique Chinese garden court inside the Metropolitan Museum of Art. That garden was modeled after the famous Peony Study of the Ming in the western garden court of the Master—of—Nets Garden.

1

2

3

4

1. 砖雕门楼
2. 大门
3. 宋刻"槃涧"
4. 引静桥与铺地
5. 殿春簃书房
6. 月到风来亭

1. A Door with Richly Carved Earthen Ornamentation
2. The Main Entrance
3. "Serene Ravine", Inscriptions on the Stone under the Song Dynasty
4. The Leading to Quietude Bridge and the Pavement
5. The Peony Study
6. The Moon Comes With Breeze Pavilion

5

6

1

2

3

4

1. 万卷堂
2. 濯缨水阁
3. 轿厅
4. 看松读画轩
5. 窗景
6. 竹外一枝轩

1. The Hall of 10, 000 Volumes
2. The Washing My Ribbon Pavilion over the Water
3. The Sedan – Chair Hall
4. The Watching Pines & Appreciating Paintings Studio
5. A Window Picture
6. The Prunus Mume Pavilion

5

6

环秀山庄

THE MOUNTAIN VILLA WITH EMBRACING BEAUTY

环秀山庄位于苏州城中景德路,面积仅0.2公顷。1988年列为全国重点文物保护单位;1997年,与拙政园、留园、网师园一起作为苏州古典园林的典型例证,被联合国教科文组织列入《世界遗产名录》。据传,园最早为宋代金谷园的一部分,明代为大学士申时行花园,清前期为尚书毕沅所有。嘉庆年,园主孙氏请叠山名家戈裕良重构花园,戈氏根据小块太湖石的自然纹理进行组合,堆叠出一座大型湖石假山,山上崖道、山洞、曲洞、石室、磴道、幽谷、峰峦、危径、绝壁等,曲折回环,宛转多姿,变幻莫测,既逼真坚固,又极尽万壑千山之妙趣,营造出一个"空山不见人"、"清泉石上流"的山水空间。戈裕良自创叠山"钩带法",环秀山庄的大假山正是这一方法的例证。假山下还有池水萦绕,山巅有古木参天;山池四周有漏窗高墙,南北有四面厅与补秋舫。置身其间,可得真山之天趣、园林之雅韵。

Located at Jing De Road, Suzhou City, the Mountain Villa with Embracing Beauty covers only 0.2 ha. In 1988 it was listed as cultural relics of national importance. Since 1997, the Mountain Villa with Embracing Beauty, the Humble Administrator's Garden, the Lingering Garden and the Master—of—Nets Garden, serving as the finest specimens of the classical gardens of Suzhou, have been inscribed on the World Heritage List by UNESCO.

It is said to be part of the Golden Valley Garden tracing far back to the Song Dynasty. During the Ming Dynasty it belonged to the Royal Academician Shen Shixing. In the early Qing Dynasty it was acquired by the Minister Bi Yuan. In the reign of Jiaqing Sun Shiyi, the owner of the garden, invited the great master Gu Yuliang to redesign the garden. By matching up the striations of numerous limestone from Lake Tai and employing the hooking techniques, he successfully re—created a magnificent range of mountains which seem to be spontaneous and uncontrived, possessing high peaks, caverns, dells, winding pathways, stone houses, stone steps, ravines, gushing spring, precipices, gullies, cliffs and the delights of wilderness. There're towering trees atop and a pool at the foot of the mountains. Enclosed by the high wall pierced with lattice windows, one finds the four—sided viewing hall to the south and the Make—Up Autumn Galley to the north, and is able to enjoy the natural beauty of "real mountains" and the charm of the true Chinese garden.

1

2

3

1. 谷口
2. 山涧
3. 山水相依
4. 悬崖
5. 廊桥

1. The Valley
2. The Ravine
3. The Mountain and Water Depend on Each Other
4. The Cliff
5. The Roofed Bridge

4

5

1

2

1. 矶岸
2. 问泉亭
3. 海棠亭
4. 飞雪崖
5. 石洞
6. 壁山

1. Rocks Projecting over the Water
2. The Putting a Question to the Spring Pavilion
3. The Malus Micromalus Makina Pavilion
4. The Gushing Spring and Precipice
5. The Cave
6. The Mountain Wall

3

4

5

6

沧浪亭

THE CANGLANG PAVILION

1

沧浪亭位于苏州古城南,占地约1.1公顷。1982年被列为江苏省文物保护单位;1998年被列入《世界遗产——苏州古典园林》增补名单。北宋庆历五年(1045),著名诗人苏舜钦遭贬至苏,购地造园,并以《楚辞·渔父》中"沧浪之水清兮,可以濯吾缨;沧浪之水浊兮,可以濯吾足"之意建沧浪亭。南宋时,园一度归韩世忠;清代起,历代地方官慕苏舜钦诗情文才,复修沧浪亭。现园中山上古木参天,山石嶙峋,北面与园外小河相傍,自然开朗,为借景之佳例;山巅沧浪亭,为清康熙年建造,亭柱上所刻"清风明月本无价,近水远山皆有情"的楹联,写出了沧浪亭的意境。园内多竹,又有清代增建的五百名贤祠,康熙皇帝御碑,文徵明石刻像,林则徐诗碑等文物古迹。

Situated in the south of the ancient city of Suzhou, the Canglang Pavilion covers 1.1 ha. In 1982 it was listed as cultural relics under the protection of Jiangsu Province. Since Dec. 1998, it has been put on A Supplemental List of the Classical Gardens of Suzhou —the World Heritage.

In the 5th year of the reign of Qingli (A. D. 1045) under the Northern Song Dynasty, the prominent poet Su Sunqin was dismissed from his post, came to Suzhou, bought a plot of land, built his garden and named a pavilion in it the Canglang Pavilion. The idea came from the Fisherman's Song in the Elegy of Chu, saying, "If the water of the Canglang River is clean, I wash the ribbon of my hat; if the water of the Canglang River is dirty, I wash my feet in it." In the Southern Song Dynasty it once belonged to Han Shizhong. Since the Qing Dynasty, local governors repaired the Canglang Pavilion several times in honor of Su Sunqin, a poetic genius. It features a range of mountains with towering age—old trees inside the garden and waterscapes skillfully borrowed from a brook on the north outside the garden. At the top of the mountain stands the Canglang Pavilion rebuilt in the reign of Kangxi under the Qing Dynasty. Parallel couplets carved on the stone pillars are intended to heighten artistic conception, reading,

"Alas! The refreshing breeze and the shining moon are priceless.

The near water and the distant mountain strike a sentimental note."

There's a variety of bamboo in the garden and a good number of cultural relics including the Temple of 500 Sages built under the Qing, Emperor Kangxi's Stelae, the Portrait of Wen Zhengming Cut on the Stone and the Stele Inscribed with Lin Zexu's Poem.

2   3

4

1. 大门
2. 沧浪胜迹石牌坊
3. 沧浪亭
4. 看山楼
5. 俞樾书"流玉"
6. 汉瓶式洞门

1. The Main Entrance
2. The Stone Archway of the Canglang Historic Place
3. The Canglang Pavilion
4. The Mountain – in – View Tower
5. Yu Yue´s Inscription "Flowing Jade"
6. Opening in the Wall Having the Shape of a Vase

5

6

1

2

3

4

1. 观鱼台与复廊
2. 林则徐书"圆灵证盟"
3. 清香馆
4. 明道堂
5. 翠玲珑

1. The Fish Watching Spot and the Double Corridor
2. Lin Zexu's Inscription "Great Confidence in the Workings of Heaven"
3. The Osmanthus Fragrans Hall
4. The Enlightenment Hall
5. The Elegant Bamboo House

5

狮子林

THE LION FOREST GARDEN

1

狮子林位于苏州古城东北隅，与拙政园相毗邻。占地1.1公顷。1982年被列为江苏省文物保护单位；1998年被列入《世界遗产——苏州古典园林》增补名单。建于元代至正二年（1342），为元末名僧惟则的弟子集资为其建造。其地原为宋代废园，多竹林怪石，有的状如狮子，又因惟则之师中峰在天目山狮子岩得法，故名。元末著名画家倪瓒（云林）曾作狮子林图。清康熙、乾隆都曾数次来游，并分别在圆明园、承德避暑山庄中仿建。狮子林有古典园林亭、台、楼、阁之胜，更以大型湖石假山群著称，被誉为"假山王国"。东北部以建筑为主，燕誉堂为典型的鸳鸯厅形式；中部水池居中，大假山横亘东西；北部有古五松园、真趣亭、暗香疏影楼等建筑；西部问梅阁侧人工瀑布从山上直泻。湖石假山群外表雄浑，内部空灵，洞壑幽深，曲折盘桓，犹如迷阵。全园结构紧凑，长廊贯通四周，曲径通幽，古树挺秀。

The Lion Forest Garden covers 1. 1 ha. and is located at the northeastern corner of the ancient city of Suzhou, adjacent to the Humble Administrator's Garden. Since Dec. 1998, it has been placed on A Supplementary List of the Classical Gardens of Suzhou —the World Heritage.

It was laid out on the site of a former Song garden in the 2nd year of the reign of Zhizheng (A.D. 1342) under the Yuan Dynasty by a group of Zen Buddhist disciples of the renowned Abbot Weize, who raised money for the construction. The garden boasts a lot of bamboo and a forest of grotesque limestone resembling lions. Hence the name. Also, Zhong Feng, the Abbot Weize's teacher, achieved enlightenment on the Lion Rock at Mt. Tianmu. By the end of the Yuan Dynasty the distinguished artist Ni Zan (Yunlin) painted a scroll of the Lion Forest Garden. The Qing emperors Kangxi and Qianlong visited it several times and made replicas of

the garden in the Yuan Ming Garden and the Imperial Mountain Resort at Chengde. Compactly yet harmoniously spaced and encircled by a long roofed walkway, the Lion Forest Garden has a prominent part for series of man—made limestone mountains, running from east to west, and pavilions, terraces and towers around a lake in the middle, and an artificial waterfall and cliffs by the Asking Prunus Mume Pavilion at the edge of the lake on the west. Various buildings here and there in clusters are to be found in the northeastern part. The Hall of Peace and Hapiness is a typical Chinese Mandarin ducks' hall. The time—honored Garden of Five Pines, the True Delight Pavilion and the Prunus Mume Tower are situated in the northern part. As the Kingdom of Rockery, the Lion Forest Garden is celebrated for its impressive and labyrinthine limestone mountains with caverns and winding pathways, old pines and cypress trees, awesome peaks and fantastic rocks.

2

3

1. 湖石假山
2. 漏窗"琴、棋、书、画"
3. 满园春色
4. 石林
5. 九狮峰

1. The Man – made Limestone Mountain
2. Latticed Windows, Shaped Like a Musical Instrument,
   Chessboard, Calligraphy and Painting
3. The Vernal Scenes of the Garden
4. The Stone Forest
5. The Nine Lions' Peak

4

5

1

2

3

雲林逸韻

4

1. 花篮厅
2. 古银杏
3. 真趣亭
4. "云林逸韵"厅
5. 立雪堂
6. 古五松园

1. The Flower Basket Hall
2. An Age – old Gingko
3. The True Delight Pavilion
4. The Hall of Yunlin's Lingering Charm
5. The Standing – in – Snow Hall
6. The Time – honored Garden Court of Five Pines

5

6

艺 圃

THE GARDEN OF CULTIVATION

1

艺圃位于苏州古城西北角吴趋坊,占地 0.38 公顷。1995 年被列为江苏省文物保护单位;1998 年被列入《世界遗产——苏州古典园林》增补名单。明天启年,大学士文震孟在袁祖庚"醉颖堂"废园遗址上建造园林。文为"明四家"文徵明曾孙,善诗画,对园精心修理后题名为药圃。清顺治年,园为姜埰所得,经修整,改名为颐园,又名敬亭山房。后又易名为艺圃,时王石谷绘有《艺圃图》。园内水池居中,各式建筑环池而筑。池北一座大型水阁延光阁横跨水面;池南为土石相间的假山,草木茂盛,小亭古树,高低相呵;山下东、西各有水湾,几架小桥,低平贴水;池东南的"乳鱼亭"为明代遗构,亭内梁枋上尚有明代彩绘。池西南"芹庐"庭院,为昔日园主读书处,精雅优美,被称为庭院精品。

Located at Wu Qu Fang in the northwestern part of the ancient city of Suzhou, the Garden of Cultivation, covering 0. 38 ha. , was laid out on the site of the ruinous Zui Ying Hall originally belonging to Yuan Zugeng in the reign of Tianqi by the Ming Royal Academician, poet and painter Wen Zhenmeng, great grandson of Wen Zhengming, one of the four great Ming painters, and was then called the Herb Garden. In the reign of Shunzhi under the Qing Dynasty, it belonged to Jiang Cai who repaired the garden and renamed it the Regimen Garden or the Mountain Villa of Jing Ting. Later on, it got its present name "the Garden of Cultivation". The great artist Wang Shigu painted a picture of the Garden of Cultivation in the early Qing Dynasty. In 1995 it was listed as cultural relics under the protection of Jiangsu Province. Since Dec. 1998, it has been put on A Supplementary List of the Classical Gardens of Suzhou—the World Heritage.

A variety of buildings are arranged around a pond in the middle of the Garden of Cultivation. To the north of the pond is the great Water Pavilion of Longevity. To the south of the pond is a range of mountains made from a mixture of earth and limestone decorated with small pavilions and luxuriant vegetation. At the foot of the mountain range there're coves on the east and west, which are spanned by low, flat and small bridges. To the southeast of the pond stands the Fry Pavilion with polychrome designs on beams and rafters dating back to the Ming Dynasty. To the southwest of the pond is a cluster of the former owner's elegant studies, called the Humble Huts, with garden courts of great excellence.

2

3

1. 乳鱼亭
2. 山水景观
3. 延光阁
4. "浴鸥"庭院
5. "浴鸥"庭院

1. The Fry Pavilion
2. The Scenic Splendors of the Garden
3. The Longevity Pavilion
4. "Bathing Gull", a Mini – garden
5. "Bathing Gull", a Mini – garden

4

5

1

1. 博雅堂
2. 香草居
3. 鹤柴
4. 明代石桥
5. 山水相间
6. 响月廊

1. The Hall of Erudition and Elegance
2. The Fragrant Herb House
3. The Crane – coop
4. The Stone Bridge Dating from the Ming
5. The Landscape and Waterscape
6. The Roofed Walkway for the Enjoyment of Moonlit Scenes

2

3

4

5

6

耦 园

THE COUPLE'S GARDEN RETREAT

耦园位于苏州城东小新桥巷内,一面临街,三面环水,占地0.8公顷。1995年被列为江苏省文物保护单位;1998年被列入《世界遗产——苏州古典园林》增补名单。最早建于清雍正年,名涉园;同治年,安徽巡抚、代理两江总督沈秉成得园重修,扩建西部,形成东、西为园,住宅居中的格局,并名园为"耦",既是两园相连的写照,也寓有沈氏夫妇双双偕隐之意。30年代初,女教育家杨荫榆在园中办"二乐女子学社";国学大师钱穆也曾在园中潜心治学;40年代,史学家顾颉刚曾借住园中研读。现东部有城曲草堂、双照楼、听橹楼、吾爱亭等景点建筑,西部有织帘老屋、藏书楼等。大型黄石假山横亘东部,山势陡峭挺拔,山形雄浑厚重,手法自然逼真,专家疑为明代叠山名家张南阳的遗作。水阁山水间内的鸡翅木透雕松竹梅"岁寒三友"落地罩,高3.5米,跨度达4米,为苏州古典园林建筑装修的精品。

Surrounded by the canal from three sides, the Couple's Garden Retreat lies in Xiao Xin Qiao Lane at the east end of the city of Suzhou, covering 0.8 ha. In 1995 it was listed as cultural relics under the protection of Jiangsu Province. Since Dec. 1998, it has been put on A Supplementary List of the Classical Gardens of Suzhou — the World Heritage.

Originally called the She Garden, it was built as early as the reign of Yongzheng under the Qing Dynasty. In the reign of Guangxu, Shen Bincheng, governor of Anhui, Jiangsu and Jiangxi, had it repaired and expanded. The housing complex on a north — south axis was flanked by the East Garden and the West Garden to contain an allusion to "Couple's Garden Retreat". Hence the name. In 1932 Yang Yinyu, an educator, established Er Yue Girls' School here. The famous Chinese scholar Qian Mu abode in the East Garden and was engaged in literary research in 1939, so did the eminent historian Gu Jiegang in the 1940s. The Old House with Woven Curtains and the Library Tower are to be found in the West Garden. Chief buildings in the East Garden include the Thatched Cottage at the City Corner, the Sun & Moon Tower, the Listening to Sculling Boats Tower, and the My Lovable Pavilion. A magnificent range of yellowstone mountains in the East Garden is believed to be piled up by the great master Zhang Nanyang in a way true to nature at the end of the Ming Dynasty. Made of ormosia wood, the circular door frame of the Amongst Mountains & Water Pavilion, about 4 m. across and 3.5 m. high, was carved in the Ming with an open — work picture of "Three Friends in the Dead of Winter", namely pine, bamboo and prunus mume instinct with life, an art treasure of this sort in the classical gardens of Suzhou.

1

2

3

1. 织帘老屋
2. "山水间"内鸡翅木飞罩
3. "山水间"水阁
4. 黄石假山·山涧
5. 黄石假山·山洞

1. The Old House with Woven Curtains
2. The Carved Ormosia Door Frame in the Pavilion of Amongst the Mountains and Water
3. The Pavilion of Amongst the Mountains and Water
4. The Ravine of the Man – made Yellowstone Mountains
5. The Cavern of the Man – made Yellowstone Mountains

4

5

1

2

3

4

1. 载酒堂
2. 还砚斋
3. "枕波双隐"廊
4. 城曲草堂
5. 东园一角
6. 藏书楼

1. The Carrying Wine Hall
2. The Return – to – Inkslab Study
3. The Roofed Walkway Called the Hermit Couple's Pillow of the Waves
4. The Thatched Cottage at the City Corner
5. A Corner of the East Garden
6. The Library Tower

5

6

退思园

THE RETREAT & REFLECTION GARDEN

退思园位于吴江同里镇,距苏州古城18公里。占地0.65公顷。1988年被列为江苏省文物保护单位。1998年被列入《世界遗产——苏州古典园林》增补名单。园建于光绪十一年(1885),安徽凤颍六泗兵备道任兰生被革职回乡,购地造园,取《左传》"进思尽忠,退思补过"句,名园退思。园自西而东,横向布局,依次为迎客区、住宅区、庭院区、山水花园。东部花园水池居中,各式建筑皆低矮轻巧,贴水而筑。主厅"退思草堂"坐北向南,隔池对景为楼廊、辛台、孤雨生凉轩等一组建筑,高低错落,虚实相间,疏密有致。池西船舫"闹红一舸"突出水面,恍如在水中航行;池东湖石假山上"眠云亭"高卧,倒影水中,与蓝天白云、绿叶红鱼构成了一幅水天一色的图画,故被誉为"贴水园"。

1

The Retreat & Reflection Garden covers 0.65 ha. and is located at the township of Tongli, Wujiang, about 18 km. away from the ancient city of Suzhou. In 1988 it was listed as cultural relics under the protection of Jiangsu Province. Since Dec. 1998 it has been put on A Supplementary List of the Classical Gardens of Suzhou — the World Heritage.

Impeached and removed from office, Ren Lansheng, commander of the military forces of Feng Ying Liu Si in Anhui, returned home, built his garden during the 11th to the 13th year of the reign of Guangxu (A.D. 1885—A.D. 1887) under the Qing Dynasty, borrowed the idea from "Zuo Zhuan", a Chinese classic, and named it the Retreat & Reflection Garden, meaning, "Advance to dedicate my loyalty to the service of my country; Retreat to reflect on mending my way." The Retreat & Reflection Garden is composed of the reception area, housing complex, garden courts and a garden which are aligned on a west — east axis. Multifarious buildings, small but delicate, are all constructed close to the pure expanse of a lake. For this reason, it is also known as the Waterscape Garden. With a southern aspect, the Thatched Hall of Retreat & Reflection, the chief building of the garden, faces over the lake a group of buildings including the Celestial Bridge, the Hardship Terrace, and the Zizania Rain Brings Coolness Pavilion, which are spaced and arranged with very great skill, having alternated the decorative with the functional or the abstract with the concrete. To the west of the lake is a "Secular Boat", a structure jotting out over the water, which looks as though moving forward on the lake. The Sleeping Cloud Pavilion stands at the top of the limestone mountain silhouetted against the blue sky with some white clouds and mirrored in the lake with lilies and goldfish forming picturesque scenes.

2

3

1. 坐春望月楼
2. 退思草堂
3. 雾中山水
4. 退思草堂内景
5. 楼廊

1. The Lasting Spring and Moon Viewing Tower
2. The Thatched Hall of Retreat & Reflection
3. The Misty Landscape and Waterscape
4. The Interior of the Thatched Hall of Retreat & Reflection
5. The Corridor of the Tower

4

5

1

1. 菰雨生凉轩
2. 眠云亭
3. 绿掩楼台
4. "清风明月"长廊
5. 闹红一舸
6. 水天一色

1. The Zizania Rain Brings Coolness Pavilion
2. The Sleeping Cloud Pavilion
3. The Towers and Terraces Partially Concealed by Trees
4. The Roofed Walkway Called "the Refreshing Breeze and the Bright Moon"
5. "A Secular Boat"
6. The Sky and Water are of One Color

2

3

4

5

6